Thatcham

in old picture postcards

by
Peter Allen
and
John Hutchings

European Library - Zaltbommel/Netherlands MCMLXXXIII

GB ISBN 90 288 2339 5

European Library in Zaltbommel/Netherlands publishes among other things the following series:

IN OLD PICTURE POSTCARDS is a series of books which sets out to show what a particular place looked like and what life was like in Victorian and Edwardian times. A book about virtually every town in the United Kingdom is to be published in this series. By the end of this year about 75 different volumes will have appeared. 1,250 books have already been published devoted to the Netherlands with the title In oude ansichten. In Germany, Austria and Switzerland 500, 60 and 15 books have been published as In alten Ansichten; in France by the name En cartes postales anciennes and in Belgium as En cartes postales anciennes and/or In oude prentkaarten 150 respectively 400 volumes have been published.

For further particulars about published or forthcoming books, apply to your bookseller or direct to the publisher.

This edition has been printed and bound by Grafisch Bedrijf De Steigerpoort in Zaltbommel/Netherlands.

INTRODUCTION

Thatcham has a long and interesting history, much more extensive than that of the nearby town of Newbury, which has eclipsed it today. It is now one of the many parishes of the Newbury District in the county of Berkshire — fifth largest in area, Thatcham is the second largest in population. Just a hundred years ago, however, things were very different. In the nineteenth century, Thatcham was an agricultural community with an identifiable nucleus centred on its village green. In the twentieth century it is a small town, characterised by ribbon development, new residential estates and growing light industry.

On a longer time-scale, even more changes have occurred in Thatcham. Ten thousand years ago, Thatcham was the site of an encampment of Mesolithic peoples. It was occupied on and off for several centuries: its inhabitants hunted the wild animals then found in the area and used flints to light fires to cook their food and to make tools and weapons. The site has now been systematically excavated — it is the only British site where large quantities of animal bones have been found in conjunction with a well developed flint industry.

The Romans built a settlement at Thatcham almost two thousand years ago. The site has not been satisfactorily identified, but some authorities believe that it may actually be 'Spinae', a military station known to have been located on the Roman road from Silchester to the west. Certainly it was a sizeable place containing civilians as well as soldiers. Scattered evidence of villas and workshops has been unearthed along with such items as pottery, coins and jewellery. The Roman settlement seems to have declined after about the year 375 A.D.

The Saxons came to Thatcham after the Romans left and it is presumed that it was one of their leaders, named 'Tace', who gave the place the name of 'Tace's-ham' (Thatcham). Nothing is known of Tace beyond this but in the will of a later Saxon chief, named Aelfeah, is found the earliest extant written reference to Thatcham, dated about 971 A.D. Further documentary information is available from the celebrated Domesday Book of 1086 A.D. This source reveals that Norman Thatcham was a relatively prosperous place: with a population of perhaps 250 people, it was held before and after the Conquest by the kings of England.

Thatcham remained a royal estate until 1123 or thereabouts when it was granted to the newly created Reading Abbey. Under the Abbey's patronage,

Thatcham reached the peak of its mediaeval development. It was one of the four main boroughs of Berkshire (along with Windsor, Wallingford and Reading) by the fourteenth century. From the time of King Henry I at least, Thatcham had a weekly market and an annual fair was held from the year 1222 onwards. In 1306 Thatcham was first taxed as a borough.

Later in the fourteenth century, Thatcham's prosperity began to falter, probably in the face of the challenge posed by the emergence of Newbury. When the monastic houses were dissolved during the reign of King Henry VIII in the sixteenth century, Reading Abbey was no longer able to protect Thatcham. From that time on, the place reverted to village status — a situation which prevailed until the latter twentieth century. Most of the subsequent history of Thatcham has been played out in the shadow of Newbury's rise to ascendancy.

Indeed, for almost two centuries, from 1540 until 1720, Thatcham was owned by the Winchcombe family, descendants of the famous 'Jack o'Newbury'. Then, in the eighteenth century, Thatcham became the property of the Waring family who actually took up residence in the place. They had a fine manor house — 'Dunston House' — built in parkland to the north of the village centre. But their stay was short-lived and their manor house was demolished about 1799; thereafter, Thatcham once again had non-resident lords of the manor.

In the nineteenth and early twentieth centuries, life in Thatcham went on much as in any other English village. There was a daily round of work to be done, punctuated by occasional holidays and festivities. Most of the Victorian and Edwardian history of Thatcham was enacted on and around the village green in the Broadway. The inhabitants lived and worked in houses and businesses in or near 'Broad Street'; whenever appropriate, they assembled on the green itself to celebrate one event or another.

There were fewer than 3,000 inhabitants in Thatcham at the end of the nineteenth century but changes were imminent. The population, still well below 5,000 in 1950, rose to 10,000 by 1970 and was approaching 15,000 in 1980. The inhabitants of Thatcham a century ago would hardly recognise the place today. Fortunately, present and future generations may glean some idea of the Thatcham which has now been 'lost' from the collection of photographs in this book.

1. This was the scene that greeted travellers on the Bath Road as they approached Thatcham from the west. Here, Turnpike Road joins the main road on the left of the picture. The road through Thatcham was 'turnpiked' about 1720 and roadusers then had to pay a toll — the road was heavily used and income from the Thatcham toll-gate was considerable. There was a gate across the road in front of the toll-house until 1878. The toll-house (on the right) and cottage, as shown here in about 1930, remained inhabited for many years afterwards and were only demolished in 1965.

2. After the toll-gate, there were few other houses on the Bath Road before the centre of Thatcham — over a mile away — until the twentieth century. The houses shown here (numbers 81 to 93, Bath Road) stand on the north side of the road. They are built over the Roman road, which once followed a similar course to the modern road at this point. These houses are substantially-built residences, and some of them have the dates of their construction recorded on stones in their walls — for instance, the house on the extreme right was built in 1904. This photograph dates from about 1910.

3. This photograph, of the 1920's, shows Northfield Road, which runs north off the Bath Road. The former road was once known by the soubriquet 'Three Chimney Lane' from the fact that some cottages — with three chimneys — stood at the end of the lane near its junction with the Bath Road. The new name 'Northfield Road' was officially adopted as early as 1896 by Mr. T.H. Brown, one of Thatcham's first parish councillors. In this view, local builder Mr. F. Reynolds poses beside an open trench in which some work is being undertaken by his men, probably connected with water supply.

4. Here, on a site just to the east of Northfield Road, Mr. F. Reynolds is seen again. He is standing next to an important discovery which his workmen made, whilst digging the foundations for new houses, in what was then a field. A Roman well was excavated and found to contain — among other things — this circular piece of stone, about two and a half feet long and a foot in diameter. It was at first thought to have been a Roman milestone, but was later identified as part of a stone column, perhaps intended for a grand house in Silchester, but abandoned when broken in transit along the Roman road.

5. Cold Ash is located on the top of a ridge about a mile up Northfield Road. This view, looking north past 'the schools', is of about 1920. In the left foreground — outside St. Mark's Church — is the lychgate erected at the instigation of the Reverend Walter Grindle, vicar of Cold Ash. The parish clerk, Mr. J.R. Staniford, complained that the gate stood too far out into the road and, later, it had to be set further back. The school — which was opened in 1874 — can be seen behind the lychgate; it still functions as an Anglican school today. In the distance is the house now named 'Honeysuckle Cottage'.

6. This is the Cold Ash hospital, depicted as it was about 1903. It was built and opened in 1892 as a 'cottage hospital' and its patients were all children — one of them can be seen (centre) on crutches. Many of the hospital's patients were city children who came to convalesce at Cold Ash. The hospital was surrounded by fir trees, which were thought to be beneficial to respiratory illnesses, but in September 1933 the woodland caught fire and the hospital had to be temporarily evacuated! Cold Ash hospital was closed down completely in 1964 and the building was demolished around 1970.

7. Just off the road leading up to Cold Ash today, in Collaroy Road, is 'St. Finian's Farm'. This photograph shows farmer Robert Law (see picture number 8) outside the farm in 1895. At that time the road was called New Road and the farm was known as 'Holder's Farm'. (Earlier in the nineteenth century it had been owned by farmer James Holder.) About 1930, after it had become the property of the Fitzwilliam family, the farm was enlarged and renamed 'St. Finian's'. In her old age, Lady Alice Fitzwilliam was cared for by nuns: after her death, the family property passed to them and they still own much of it now.

8. This photograph was also taken at 'St. Finian's' (Holder's Farm) in 1895. Farmer Robert Law is seen here (right foreground) helping his labourers with the haymaking. He was born in Fifeshire, Scotland, in 1832 and worked as head gardener and steward on several estates in the north of England and Hampshire before coming to Cold Ash around 1877. Returning from Newbury market one day in January, 1897, with his horse and cart, he was suddenly taken ill and assisted on his way home. Tragically, he fell from the cart as it stood in the farmyard and died from the injuries he sustained.

Newtown
Thatcham A 384

9. Back on the main Bath Road, beyond Northfield Road towards the centre of
Thatcham, more imposing residences were built early in the present century. These
houses (numbers 11 to 43, Bath Road) also stand on the north side of the main road.
Again, some of them have the dates of their construction recorded in their brickwork —
the pair on the left were erected in 1906, for instance. Interestingly, when these houses
were being built, Roman wells were found on their sites. This photograph, of about 1910,
shows the main Bath Road through Thatcham in a very different condition to that which
prevails today, now that it carries a large volume of traffic.

10. On the south side of the Bath Road, opposite the houses shown in the last picture, was Thatcham 'Newtown'. It was served by its own public house, the 'Black Horse' in St. John's Road. In this photograph, several of the customers have taken their drinks outside to pose for the camera. Seated in the centre of the front row is Charles James the landlord – the James family kept the 'Black Horse' from about 1910 until 1967. All the decorations adorning the premises indicate that the photograph was taken on the occasion of the coronation of King George V in June, 1911.

11. This view, dating from the early years of the century, can no longer be seen today. It shows a row of cottages which were demolished about 1961. They stood at the bottom of Green Lane — which runs south off the Bath Road — where Crown Acre Close has been built since. The cottages were known as 'Green Lane Terrace' and stood on land owned by the Wallis family, who farmed nearby at 'Thatcham Farm'. An adjacent range of houses, at right-angles to Green Lane itself and still standing today, was named 'Hollington Place' by Farmer Wallis's wife, after the farm where she had been born.

12. Returning to the main Bath Road, this house — photographed here around 1914 — stands almost opposite the junction with Green Lane. A listed building, 'The Poplars' is an eighteenth century house which has been extensively modified over the years. It was once the home of the Baily family, but not of Francis Baily, the celebrated astronomer, himself — his uncle sold the property in about 1816. The building is an interesting example of a 'lobby entry' house: the original lobby entry can still be seen in the brickwork at the front of the house, although it has since been replaced by a window.

13. This was the approach to the village proper, looking east, as it was about 1930. On the left, behind the fence, was a garden and a house named 'The Ferns' where Mr. Joseph Lane ran a private school — the modern relief road (opened in 1962) runs right across it today! The one-time main road, now simply the High Street, winds on to the centre of the village, past a crossroads in this photograph (note the road sign in the middle distance). The crossroads was formed by the intersection of the old main road with Church Lane (on the right) and Park Lane (on the left), which now leads off the relief road instead.

High St.
Thatcham   A 360

14. Like the previous picture, this view shows the High Street again, although the date is rather earlier — probably about 1914 — and here a little closer to the village centre. The entrance to Church Lane can be seen on the right, just behind the boy on the bicycle. On the left, where the girl is standing, are the premises of Norris the fishmonger. By the mid-1930's, this narrow section of road — then still the main road from London to the West — had become a notorious bottle-neck, and Norris's shop was demolished in August 1934, to allow the road to be widened.

15. The British School (left) and Independent (now United Reformed) Church (right) still stand in Church Lane today. The school was built in 1847 and the church in 1804. When the Independent Church opened, angry opponents of nonconformity in Thatcham burned an effigy of John Barfield, the man who had made the opening possible. Early congregations at the church were accompanied to services to the sound of 'music' being played on pots and kettles! The only change which has occurred in the seventy or so years since this photograph was taken is that the railings in front of the old school have now disappeared.

16. The British School in Church Lane functioned as such from 1847 until 1913. In March, 1882, Mr. Horatio Barton Skillman took over as schoolmaster and proved to be both a popular and successful teacher. He is shown in this photograph as a relatively young man, in about the year 1890, with some of his pupils, outside the British School premises. In 1913, Mr. Skillman, with his staff and pupils, transferred to the (then) new Council School in the London Road. Mr. Skillman continued to teach in Thatcham until December 1922, when he had reached the official retirement age.

17. This cottage still stands immediately opposite the British School in Church Lane. It is named 'Monks' Chambers': it is only a few yards from the parish church, but it is doubtful whether any monks ever really lived here, although there may have been an earlier building on the same site. The present building dates in origin to about 1500 A.D. and there is still some wattle and daub in its roof. During the nineteenth century 'Monks' Chambers' served as the coachman's cottage for the 'Priory', a large residence nearby. The cottage — shown here early in this century — has been carefully renovated today.

PARK LANE THATCHAM. 194?

18. This photograph shows the view looking north up Park Lane in the 1920's. At the time, Park Lane — once known by the less attractive name of 'Back Lane' — led directly off the High Street. The houses which can be seen on the right of the picture have changed little today. One of them, in the distance, was called 'Wetherdene' and was the home of Mr. Arthur Brown. In 1923, his daughter, Marjorie, opened a private preparatory school in a small schoolroom in the (then) meadow on the left of the photograph. It closed in 1951 and modern houses have since been built in the meadow.

19. This is a photograph of one of Thatcham's old family businesses, and is reliably dated to 1892. It shows the premises, on the south side of the High Street, of William Golding Lay. Mr. Lay (on the right) came to Thatcham from Wantage and took over an established grocery business in 1871; he ran it until his death in 1905. Thereafter, his wife (centre) and three sons (one of them, Hubert, is shown here, on the left) kept the business going as a family concern until 1933. Although in different ownership today, the premises still function as a shop and are now a greengrocery business.

CHURCH PARADE THATCHAM 18.8.12

20. More business premises in the High Street can be seen in this picture, which is clearly dated 18 August, 1912. However, the major focus of interest is the Church Parade — making its way along the street — held that Sunday. The parade was arranged by local old soldiers who had formed themselves into a 'National Reserve', and were supported by Oddfellows and other friendly societies. Among those in the parade were National Reservists' bands from Reading and Hungerford as well as the Thatcham brass band. Two banners of the 'Jack o'Newbury' Lodge of Oddfellows were carried and one of them can be seen here.

21. From the end of the High Street, looking back in the direction of Newbury (west), this was the scene around the turn of the century. The position of the shadows and the fact that several of the shops on the north side of the street have their blinds down, suggests that it is a hot summer's afternoon. On the left is the inn sign of the 'White Hart' and opposite are the premises of the Brooks family, cornmerchants; the tall shops next door have now been demolished and replaced by modern developments. In the distance are some of the 'vehicles' which then used the streets of Thatcham.

gh St Thatcham
C456.

22. This photograph portrays the same scene as the previous one, but dates from some years later, probably about 1914. The centre of interest here — for the village children too — is the early motor car. It is reputed to be one of the first cars owned by a local person and belonged to Mr. J.M. Henry, whose family then kept Colthrop Paper Mill. The vehicle was an open-topped Argyle. Mr. Henry, appropriately attired, can be seen standing nearby, talking to Mr. Wyatt, the butcher. The solitary car shown here presents a marked contrast to the scene in the High Street today!

23. Another of Thatcham's early motor cars is shown in this photograph of about the same time as the previous one. The car is a 3½ horse-power Benz: it had a rear engine, was chain-driven and completely open to the elements. This particular vehicle was built about 1902. The car was driven from the left hand side — here, the driver is Mr. Charles George Brown, Snr. (see pictures 59 and 60), seen with his daughter May. Although the location of the photograph is uncertain, it was probably taken at the back of Brown's premises on the north side of the High Street.

24. Late in the last century and in the early part of the present century, Thatcham was served by two saddlers and harness-makers from premises at opposite ends of the High Street. One of them, located where the main road curved round into Chapel Street, was established by George Ashman. The business was carried on after his death by his sons. Shown here, in a view of about 1920, are brothers Frank (on the extreme left) and Sydney Ashman (right), with employees Dick (inner left) and Frank Harding (centre), posing with a fine display of their wares. Their shop was not finally demolished until the 1950's.

25. This photograph of the early 1920's shows the original premises — at the western end of Chapel Street — of the Thatcham Road Transport Service. In 1921 Sydney Ashman and Wilfred Street joined forces to set up T.R.T.S., a road haulage company. They operated from this yard until about 1924, when the business was transferred to Colthrop, but their lorries were still a familiar sight on local roads. In later years, the square building (right) served as Reg Smart's fish and chip shop until it was demolished in 1962 to make way for the new relief road; the 'garage' (left) still stands today.

26. There were occasions when T.R.T.S. found that operating a fleet of delivery vehicles — even a small one — was not without its problems. This photograph shows what happened to one T.R.T.S. vehicle during a journey to London in July, 1929. The Sentinel steam wagon fell into a trench beside the road on the A 4. at Colnbrook — it was later recovered, of course! T.R.T.S. started up in business in Thatcham with just one vehicle in 1921. After the business moved to Colthrop a fleet of about a hundred lorries was gradually built up, and became the 'Colthrop Transport Company' in 1954.

CHAPEL STREET, THATCHAM.

27. This was the scene looking east along Chapel Street towards Reading in about the year 1910. The only 'vehicle' in sight is a horse and cart in the distance — very different from today, as this is still part of the main road and now carries a considerable volume of motor traffic. Of the buildings shown in the photograph, those in the left foreground are still extant, but the one in the centre (with the 'stepped' end) has since been demolished. The next four pictures feature buildings which stand, or once stood, on the north side of Chapel Street in this general area.

28. Set back from the road in Chapel Street is the Wesleyan Methodist Church, seen here as it was in about 1914. The building was converted from an old brush turnery works and was first used as a church in 1834. It was originally completely closed in by cottages, and was approached through a narrow passageway, but they were demolished later in the nineteenth century. In their place lawns were laid and laurel trees were planted. Today, the ivy has been removed from the front of the church, which is still used as a place of worship by local Methodists.

29. These were some of the cottages which once stood near the Methodist Church — they were known as the 'Nine Shilling Houses', presumably because this was once the annual rental paid by their inhabitants. They were old charity cottages, of which Thatcham once had many. The row comprised four part-thatched-part-tiled cottages (numbers 22 to 28, Chapel Street), with drop-leaf shutters at the windows. Also shown, at the extreme left, is a single cottage (number 20) with a fully thatched roof. By the turn of the century — the date of this photograph — the cottages had fallen into disrepair.

30. This is another view of the 'Nine Shilling Houses', looking west along Chapel Street to where the road curved around to the left into the High Street. This photograph shows numbers 22-28, Chapel Street, after they had been repaired in 1901. The thatch has been replaced entirely by tiles; the window shutters have been removed; and a new dormer has been added to number 28 (compare the previous picture). New guttering has been fitted to the houses and their general appearance enhanced. They remained inhabited until they were demolished and modern police houses were built on their site in 1967.

31. At the western end of the 'Nine Shilling Houses', a completely new building appeared early in the present century. The old thatched cottage (number 20, Chapel Street) was sold to Berkshire County Council for £150 in 1904 and demolished to make way for Thatcham's police station. The building was occupied during the summer of 1905 — it had offices and one cell on the ground floor and living accommodation for the sergeant-in-charge above. The police station is shown here as it was soon after opening; it remained in use as such until 1969, but will shortly revert to police use.

32. A number of the local children have posed for the photographer here. However, his intention was probably to take a picture of the building behind them — the Parish Hall, on the south side of Chapel Street. The hall was built at the instigation of Miss A.L. Henry, the third daughter of John Henry of Colthrop — a stone set in the front wall of the building commemorates the part she played in its construction. The work was done by Mr. W. Child, a Thatcham builder. The village hall was erected in 1907, being officially opened in April of that year, and was still quite new when this picture was taken.

33. In this photograph — looking west along Chapel Street to the centre of Thatcham — an array of buildings on the north side of the road can be seen. The 'Nine Shilling Houses' are in the distance (extreme left) in this view of about 1914. Like them, the pair of houses in the foreground have gone today; they were demolished to make way for the access road into the Park Avenue estate in the early 1960's. The houses were quite interesting architecturally — they had halfhipped roofs with tile-hung ends — but this did not prevent them from suffering the same fate as many other old houses in Thatcham!

34. This picture was taken from almost the same place as the previous one, probably at about the same date. However, this is the view looking east along Chapel Street, out of the village. The same row of houses occupy the (left-hand) foreground in this photograph, as in the last one, with another array of buildings beyond them. On the right, behind the fence, is the piece of open land — 'Turnfield' — which was sold to the parish council by Mr. Arthur Brown for the purpose of setting up a children's playground. Yet another new road has now been completed and crosses part of Turnfield to join the main road at this point today.

35. These are virtually the only thatched houses remaining in Thatcham — the 'Thatched Cottages' (numbers 66-74, Chapel Street). They are seventeenth century origin, built with timber frames and brick-infilling, and were once charity cottages. By the early twentieth century they were in a dilapidated state, but they were renovated at a cost of £560 in 1930 and let at low rents to poor families. In 1973-74, the five cottages were converted into four and sold to private owners. Today each cottage is a listed building in its own right: they are shown here as they were about 1914.

36. This is a view of the south side of Chapel Street, looking west, in or around 1890. On the left is the 'New Inn', which still functions as a public house nearly a century later although it was renamed the 'Prancing Horse' in 1968. Next to the inn is Loundyes' almshouse: there has been an almshouse on this site since the fifteenth century, but the building shown here was built in 1849 (and has been further modified since). Chapel Street itself can be seen as it was before a proper road surface was laid; it is virtually traffic-free in this view, a far cry from today!

37. On the opposite (north) side of Chapel Street to that shown in the previous picture, this was the scene in the early years of the present century. The photograph shows the junction of the main road with the road to Bucklebury, off to the left. In the foreground 'Marsh House' can be seen: dating from the eighteenth century, the house has been the home of some notable local families. Although it was a listed building, the house was demolished in 1972 and its site remains empty today. Partially hidden by the tree is 'Bluecoats', the house where the schoolmaster at the Bluecoat School (on the right) used to live.

38. Thatcham has some three dozen listed buildings but this photograph shows its only grade one example. The building dates from the year 1304 and was originally a chanty chapel. It retains some ecclesiastical features, such as the niches (which once held religious statues) on either side of the doorway. The chapel remained in use until the middle of the sixteenth century, when it was suppressed during the Reformation. It is shown here in the early years of the twentieth century — the brick wall (left), wooden fence and gas lamp have all disappeared today, but the building itself stands and is presently used as an antique shop.

39. This is another view of the old chapel, showing the building from the east, in the year 1924. Again, some of its ecclesiastical features can be identified — for example, the small priest's door in the south wall. After lying empty for a century and a half, the old chapel was taken over as a schoolroom in 1707 and functioned as such — being known as the 'Bluecoat School' — until 1914. The last schoolmaster was Mr. Samuel Vallis, who lived at the adjoining house; it can be seen immediately behind the school, with 'Marsh House' beyond. In this photograph, a signpost has appeared at the road junction by the school.

40. The road up the hill to Bucklebury — like the main road from which it leads — is very busy with traffic today. In the early years of this century, when this photograph was taken, it was clearly much quieter! At the point shown in the picture, the road is passing Hart's Hill Farm, which was kept for many years by the Adnams family. In 1888, workmen digging for gravel by the roadside on Hart's Hill discovered three beautiful urns — further evidence of the Roman occupation of the locality. Today, the road from Thatcham up the hill to Bucklebury is known as 'Hartshill Road'.

41. Back on the main road, this was the view looking east towards Reading in 1915. On the right is another of Thatcham's old inns, the 'Plough'. Alongside, the white railings (now long-since gone) mark the entrance to Stoney Lane. Beyond are two houses which still stand today although the furthest one has now been incorporated into a modern restaurant. In the distance is the Council School, on the 'London Road'. In the foreground of the photograph is the large green — still known as the Marsh — showing the pond which was filled in for health reasons during the 1930's.

42. This photograph, of about the same date as the previous one, shows the main road looking west back into the centre of Thatcham. In the foreground is the 'Plough' inn again — advertising its ales and stouts from the now defunct Aldermaston Brewery — and the railings at the top of Stoney Lane. Beyond is a row of 'double-pile' houses named 'Park View' from the fact that from them — across the Marsh to the right — it is possible to see where Dunston Park and its mansion house used to stand in the eighteenth century. In the distance, along Chapel Street, the Bluecoat School is just visible.

43. Today, there are petrol stations and garages all along the modern main road, to cater for the vehicles using it. This photograph shows how one of them began: this is he 'Rose Garage' in London Road, Thatcham, as it was about 1930. It was then kept by the brothers Robinson (shown here in front of their premises), who advertised 'an easy pull-in, convenient oil cabinets, electric pumps and well-equipped workshop'. Nowadays the garage has been replaced by the less-quaintly named 'Station Supreme', and the Robinson's premises have disappeared under the forecourt of a large self-service petrol station.

44. The 'Council School' was built on a new site south of the London Road at the eastern extremity of Thatcham. The school was built for Berkshire County Council at a cost of £4,000 and opened on 1st April, 1913. This photograph of the school was taken around that date – it shows the turret, on the roof of the building, from which a bell was hung to call the village children to school each day. In the first week after it opened, nearly two hundred children enrolled at the school, among them all of the pupils from the over-crowded British School in Church Lane (see picture number 16).

45. In this photograph some of the Council School pupils and two of their teachers have posed for the camera. The picture shows a group of 'infant' children (aged from five to seven years) with teachers Miss Rhoda Pearce (back row left) and her niece Miss Minnie Pearce (back row right). Like Mr. Skillman the headmaster, Rhoda Pearce had transferred to the Council School from the British School in 1913. This photograph was taken in about 1920 — sadly, Rhoda Pearce died in June, 1921, having been a teacher of little children in Thatcham for forty years. Some of the infants pictured here are now local pensioners!

46. This photograph was taken inside the Council School in about 1927. The building then contained six classrooms and the one shown here was also the school hall. The pupils, comprising 'Class I', were (then) the 'top' group — aged around thirteen, they would have started work at the end of the academic year. Their teachers are the four adults standing at the back of the room. Third from the left is Mr. Cox, who succeeded Mr. Skillman as headmaster in 1922. The other three are (from left to right) Miss Stanbrook, Miss Hart and Arthur Collins, all of whom were 'pupil-teachers' at the school.

On the Canal.
Thatcham.

47. This photograph — 'on the canal' at Thatcham — was actually taken at Colthrop during the early years of the century. The Kennet and Avon Canal was completed throughout from Reading to Bath in 1810. This section of the canal, however (from Reading to Newbury only), had been opened in 1723 by making cuts in the River Kennet to improve its navigability. Here, the canal passed under a wooden swingbridge which linked Colthrop Cottages (on the left) with Colthrop Paper Mill on the opposite bank. From the mill, a lane led up to the main road and thence back towards the centre of Thatcham or on to Reading.

48. The canal at Colthrop formed the southern boundary of the site of the Colthrop Paper Mill, shown here at about the same date as the previous photograph. There had been a mill here since at least the early fifteenth century. Originally it was a corn mill, but in the eighteenth century it became a paper mill. The mill was taken over by Mr. John Henry in 1861 and remained in his family's ownership until 1918. Thereafter, the business was merged with larger concerns so that it grew into the massive complex which operates at Colthrop today. The old mill buildings shown in this view have now been demolished.

49. Colthrop's paper mill was taken over in 1918 by the London firm of Croppers. A new company — Colthrop Board and Paper Mills Ltd. — was formed on the Colthrop site in 1920. Based on the work Croppers had been doing in London, a factory was erected at Colthrop to use paper made by the mill for the manufacture of folding cardboard boxes. The interior of the factory, then known as 'Containers Ltd.', can be seen in this photograph of about 1923. The company is still very much in business today, although — following another merger in 1968 — it is now part of the 'Field' group.

50. The rapidly expanding paper mill at Colthrop experienced a number of major fires. After the London firm of Croppers assumed control of the mill in the 1920's, a fire-brigade was established on the Colthrop site. The brigade had its own fire engine, as shown here: the vehicle was a 1919 Leyland with a 'Braidwood' body and a two-stage Merryweather pump capable of pumping 350 gallons of water per minute. The vehicle was purchased second-hand from the London Fire Brigade for £80; it eventually broke down and was sold off to a Newbury scrap yard for five pounds.

51. This photograph was taken on the canal bank at a point half a mile or so west of Colthrop, near Thatcham's railway station. It shows the old wharf — on the opposite bank — and the one-time station buildings in the background. Among the station buildings (which were erected in 1892), is the original signal box (which was demolished in 1921) — hence the picture was taken between these dates. Even though Thatcham is situated on the main line from London to the West Country, its railway station has changed today: trains still stop at the platforms, but the station buildings were demolished in 1965.

52. In places, the Kennet and Avon canal utilises the course of the River Kennet itself; in other places, new channels were dug for the canal and the river was left to meander on its way. Here, in the meadows to the south of Thatcham (although not far from the paper mill and railway station), the river presents a tranquil scene in the early years of this century. In the distance is Chamberhouse Mill, which originated as a corn mill sometime in the fourteenth century and operated as such until as recently as 1965. Today, the old corn mill has been converted into private residential accommodation, but the river is still as pleasant as ever.

53. This is a view of 'Bull's Locks', about two miles to the west of the area where the previous photographs were taken. At this point, the canal and the river — having followed different courses from Newbury — join up and share the same course for a short distance. The canal enters the locks from the west (on the left) whilst the river flows in from the north. In this photograph, taken soon after the turn of the century, the lengthman's house can clearly be seen on the right of the picture, behind the 'daring young man' perched on the footbridge handrail. The house was demolished around 1946 and all trace of it has gone today.

54. From the canal and railway, a road named 'Station Road' leads back into the centre of Thatcham. Along its route is 'Thatcham House', built about 1870 and photographed here at the turn of the century. This imposing edifice was built for the family of the Reverend Hezekiah Martin. In 1902 it became the home of the Buller-Turner family, two of whose sons — Alexander and Victor — were later awarded Victoria Crosses. The house still stands today although it is now hemmed in by modern housing developments: it is no longer lived in and will soon be converted into office space instead.

55. Station Road leads back into the centre of Thatcham at the Broadway — 'Broad Street' as it used to be known, for obvious reasons! On turning the corner into the Broadway, this was the scene (looking north) as depicted in a postcard view of about 1910. The large building in the foreground served as the parish workhouse until 1837, when it was sold off and converted into a number of private dwellings. In 1959, the house was demolished and a shopping development — 'Tanner House' — was built on the site. Several of the local people have posed for the photographer here.

BROAD ST. THATCHAM. 153.

56. This picture is of the same scene as the previous one, but this time looking south, around about the same date. This is again the bottom corner of the Broadway with the old workhouse in the foreground. Beyond, the road turns the corner down to the railway station: on the left is the 'Old Chequers', still functioning as a public house today, and on the right is the now defunct turnery works. Wood turning is one of Thatcham's oldest trades and was carried on in these premises until 1958. Now, the buildings of the turnery works shown here have been demolished — like the old workhouse in the foreground.

57. The Broadway is again depicted in this view of about the turn of the century. Here, looking south from the top of the Broadway, it is possible to see the stump of Thatcham's ancient market cross marking the spot where the mediaeval markets were held. Around the cross is the original seat, erected by Samuel Barfield in 1892. In front of it is the old direction post, placed there by Stephen Pinnock in 1884, its three 'fingers' (one partially obscured) pointing the way to Reading, Newbury and Thatcham's railway station. In the distance are the turnery work's chimneys — landmarks for miles around!

58. This was the view looking north to the top of the Broadway at about the same date as the previous photograph. In the background is another tall chimney which dominated the Broadway — that of the old axle-tree foundry. The last man in Thatcham to carry on this now forgotten calling was Stephen Parr: after he retired in 1904 the foundry chimney was reduced in height as it had become unsafe. This photograph also shows (on the extreme left and the extreme right) the situation of the two premises occupied by another of Thatcham's local tradesmen, Charles George Brown, Senior (see the next two pictures).

59. These were the first premises which Mr. C.G. Brown occupied, on the north side of the Broadway at its junction with the High Street. Mr. Brown was apprenticed as a watchmaker and — after working for other watchmakers — he set up his own business here in Thatcham in 1891. Later, he also began selling and repairing bicycles from these premises. In this photograph, dating from the early years of the present century, some of his wares have been put on display outside the shop. Mr. Brown is also posing for the photograph, in the centre of the picture. Today, the premises are used by a dry-cleaning business.

60. This photograph, from the 1920's, shows 'Broadway House' on the eastern side of the Broadway. In 1917 the house became the private dwelling of the family of Arthur Henry Brown. His father, Mr. C.G. Brown, can be seen outside the house in this view; he had previously been living at the nearby motor works, but in 1927 he and his son exchanged homes. Thereafter Mr. C.G. Brown — assisted by his daughter May — ran his jewellery and watchmaking business from here until 1934 when Mr. Charles Whitehouse took the business over. In 1968 the house was demolished and replaced the following year by a new supermarket.

61. The Broadway green — the heart of Thatcham — has long been used by the inhabitants of the place for gatherings of all kinds. Here, the green is the venue for some sort of celebration — as the photograph dates from the turn of the century it must be either Queen Victoria's diamond jubilee (in June, 1897) or the coronation of King Edward VII (in August, 1902). Although there seems to be free food on offer (being delivered by the cart in the foreground), and most of the villagers are seated at tables to enjoy it, one old man at least is much more interested in having his picture taken.

62. Not all the gatherings which took place on the Broadway green involved large numbers of people — this one consists of only about thirty. The photograph dates from the early years of the present century and shows a 'camp meeting'. Precisely what this was about is not clear, but it was probably connected with the summer camps arranged by one of the local churches. The local Primitive Methodists, for example, held an annual camp meeting on the occasion of the anniversary of their Sunday School; the children of church members were normally taken to spend a few days camping in the district.

BROAD STREET.

63. This view of the Broadway green in about 1910 is actually marked with the old name 'Broad Street'. Here, an even smaller group has gathered on the green — it is perhaps a mother and her five young children? The photograph shows the road before it was tarred and metalled (in 1911) with the criss-cross of cart tracks in its surface. In the background, a tradesman — either a builder or a chimney sweep — is working on the roof of a house, with his cart parked at the foot of his ladder. Today, the whole row of houses has been demolished and a self-service supermarket built in its place.

64. This intriguing photograph was taken at the top of the Broadway in about 1910. It shows an unusual looking 'house' being transported through Thatcham by a traction engine and trailer. The building was a tall wooden structure, consisting of two rooms — one up and one down — and a staircase. Brought from outside the village, the house was delivered to a site on the corner of Henwick Lane and Bath Road. For several years, the house provided accommodation for some of the 'lady gardeners' who worked at the 'French Gardens', then kept by Miss Hughes-Jones, across the Henwick Field.

65. These next three views are all of the same thing — the 'public fountain', built at the top of the Broadway in 1911. The fountain was 'opened' to the public on the evening of the 4th July of that year. Here, the local people have turned out to witness the official 'handing over' ceremony. The fountain was built at the expense of Mrs. Ann Tomlin, an old inhabitant of Thatcham, with the permission of the parish council. Mrs. Tomlin lived her last years at 'Sydney Lodge' in Station Road and died in November, 1911, just a few months after her fountain was built and given to the people of Thatcham.

66. This photograph gives a close-up view of the south side of the fountain. The structure consisted of a shelter, with seating inside and out, and it had an attractive weather vane on the roof. A commemorative stone was set into the south wall of the shelter and recorded the fact that the fountain had been dedicated to 'King Edward the Peacemaker' (King Edward VII) and to the coronation of King George V. Interestingly, this photograph also shows the premises which C.G. Brown's sons had taken over in 1911 to establish their motor business, which the family still operates today.

67. The north side of the fountain is shown in this photograph. As well as having a public drinking fountain inside, there was a horse trough along the outside northern wall. Water for both came from a well some 140 feet deep, beneath the shelter. It was planned as an artesian well but — being so deep — a pump had to be installed to raise the water. During the mid-1930's, public toilets were built behind the fountain too. However, in 1969, both fountain and toilets were demolished and replaced the following year with 'modern' public conveniences.

68. The public fountain can be seen in the distance in this photograph, taken from the bottom of the Broadway and looking north, in about 1914. Three of the village children have posed — hoops in hand — for the camera. The photograph presents a peaceful scene, very different to that which prevails in the Broadway today. A hint of the changes to come can be detected in this picture: in the foreground is the horse and cart of one of the local carriers, but in the distance (outside Brown's garage) is an early motor lorry — among the first of many such vehicles to appear in Thatcham.

69. Another of Thatcham's early motor vehicles is shown in this photograph of about the same period. It is a Ford Model-T delivery lorry and — as it is a left-hand drive vehicle — it was probably imported from America. The vehicle belonged to Messrs. Pinnocks and is shown here in their yard on the eastern side of the Broadway. The business was started in the nineteenth century by Edmund Pinnock, who set up as a coal merchant and carrier. When Edmund died in 1898, the business was carried on by his son, Frank — shown here, arms akimbo — and still operates from the premises today.

70. This was once the scene behind the premises of the Brown brothers (sons of C.G. Brown Snr.), where they operated their motor business. The brothers had been experimenting with electric lighting and first lit their own premises, by means of some gas engines and a set of accumulators, in 1906. The gas engines were replaced by diesel engines in about 1923 and this photograph was taken shortly afterwards. Here, the brothers, Charles George Brown Jnr. (right) and Arthur Henry Brown (left), can be seen standing by the engine house; in the background (right) is the new diesel fuel tank and in the foreground (left) are water cooling tanks.

71. This is a view of the interior of the engine house where the electricity was actually generated. One of the diesel engines can clearly be seen: for the technically-minded, the engine was a Petter Hot Bulb Semi-diesel. Using their diesel engines, the Brown brothers were able to supply electricity to the village of Thatcham, at 220 volts D.C. The two brothers expanded their electricity works and were soon lighting the neighbouring shops and houses in the Broadway. In conjunction with Mr. Charles Gunter, they had formed the 'Thatcham Electric Light Works' in 1920 and soon extended their supply around the village.

72. In order to make electricity available to as many premises and homes in Thatcham as possible, it was necessary to erect poles to carry the electric wires around the village. In this picture, taken during the 1920's, nine of the men who undertook the work have posed for the photographer behind Messrs. Brown's Broadway premises. The Brown family were closely associated with the Congregational Church (see picture 15), so it is not surprising to find that the church — and the British School next door to it — were lit with electricity as early as October, 1925. Thatcham's electricity supply was nationalised in 1948.

73. This view shows the same 'Church Parade' as that depicted in an earlier photograph (number 22). Three brass bands were involved, one of which – The Reading Band of the National Reserves – had arrived in Thatcham on the morning of the parade and played on the Broadway green several times during the day. At two o'clock, members of the National Reserve lined up on the Broadway green and General E.T. Dickson presented badges to thirty-two local men. Then a procession formed – led by Provincial Grand Master Pyke and his deputy W.W. Bailey – and made its way (as shown here) to the parish church just around the corner.

74. Taken at the bottom of the Broadway, this picture shows the view west into 'Church Gate', where the parish church is situated. Although this photograph was taken some seventy years ago, it depicts one corner of Thatcham which has not changed significantly — nor is it likely to do so, for this is now designated a conservation area. All the buildings which can be seen here are still extant, even though slightly modified today. Minor changes have occurred: the chain-link fence around the 'Old Courthouse' (on the left) has now gone and the churchyard wall was reduced in height in 1936.

75. Here, the parish church is shown from the south-east, as it was in 1903. This view shows the church in its 'restored' condition, much as it appears today except that the pinnacles on the tower and the Danvers' chapel (centre foreground) have since disappeared. The church was extensively renovated in 1857-58, when parts of the exterior which had been built in red brick — such as the Danvers' chapel — were clad in flint to blend in with the rest of the church. This photograph was taken from a field, on the opposite side of Lower Way, where houses have been built today.

76. This photograph, taken from the top of the church tower, gives a 'bird's eye' view of the centre of Thatcham as it was in the early years of the twentieth century. In the middle of the picture is the old Infant School where local children were taught from 1828 to 1964. The building was demolished in 1980 and many of the other buildings around it have also gone today.

This, then, was the nucleus of the old village of Thatcham: the place has grown tremendously since most of these pictures were taken and Thatcham today is very different in character from the way it appears in this collection of views.